D1625841

Make Your Own Art

Clay Modelling

FRANKLIN WATTS
LONDON•SYDNEY

First published in 2008 by Franklin Watts

© 2008 Arcturus Publishing Limited

Franklin Watts
338 Euston Road
London NW1 3BH

Franklin Watts Australia
Level 17/207 Kent Street, Sydney, NSW 2000

Produced by Arcturus Publishing Limited,
26/27 Bickels Yard, 151–153 Bermondsey Street,
London SE1 3HA

Editor: Alex Woolf
Designers: Sally Henry and Trevor Cook
Consultant: Daisy Fearns

Picture credits: Sally Henry and Trevor Cook

A CIP catalogue record for this book is available
from the British Library.

Dewey Decimal Classification Number: 731.4′2

ISBN 978 0 7496 8188 3

Printed in China

Franklin Watts is a division of Hachette Children's Books,
an Hachette Livre UK company
www.hachettelivre.co.uk

Contents

Introduction

Some clay, a few simple tools and your imagination are all you need to have fun with modelling. In this book we use a special coloured clay called polymer clay. It's just as good as old-fashioned clay, and it comes in lots of great colours. The best part is, when you want to keep a model, you can make it hard in an ordinary oven.

Preparation

Polymer clay sticks to itself very well. It's also quite easy to stick things to it. Unfortunately, it can also stick in the wrong places. So keep it clear of expensive carpets! If there's no cooking going on, the kitchen might be the best place to work. Cover a part of the table or worktop with a plastic sheet (a plastic carrier bag is ideal). Hold it in place with sticky tape.

4

Tools

Tools like the ones below come from a craft shop. We found our rolling pin in a junior cooking set. Flat lolly sticks are free with ice lollies!

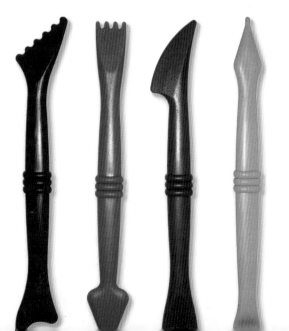

Start

Kneading the clay in your hands makes sure it's the same consistency all through. It also warms and softens the clay. Form it into a smooth ball to prepare it for rolling or forming into shapes.

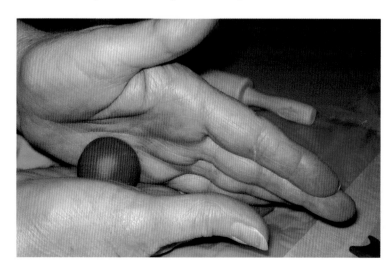

Flat sheets

Take a ball of clay and roll it out with the roller. Lolly sticks placed each side of the clay will stop the roller going down too far and help you make a clay sheet of even thickness.

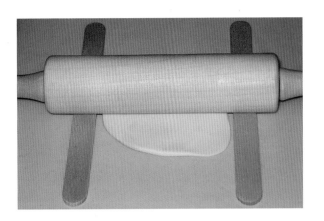

Coils

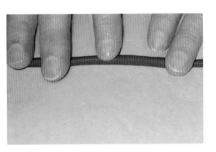

We often need long, even cylinders of clay. We call these 'coils'. Take a ball of clay and make it into a sausage shape in your hands. Put it down on the work surface and, using one hand, gently roll it into a longer, thinner shape. Use your whole hand, from wrist to fingertips. As it gets thinner, spread your fingers and try to apply even pressure. Don't rush this. See how long you can make it!

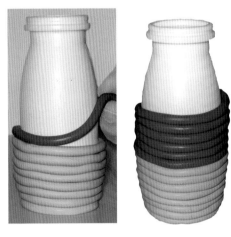

Pinching and punching

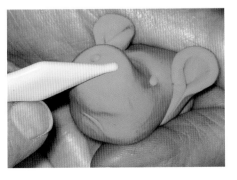

You can get a good effect by 'pinching' – squeezing clay between thumb and finger, or 'punching' – pushing something into the clay. Remember: this will distort the shape you started with.

Joining

Press pieces of clay together to make them stick. Rolling different colours together will make stripes that won't come apart. It's easy to stick flat pieces to each other.

Shape cutters

You can buy cutters like these for a few pennies. You can also find things that work just as well for nothing! Try small plastic lids.

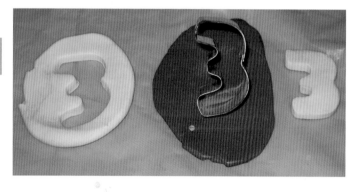

Making marks

The surface of your model doesn't have to be smooth. Try out the effects you get with different tools.
Don't be afraid of experimenting.
Ask before you borrow things from the kitchen!

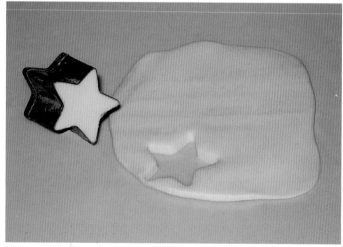

These marks and textures were made with these simple tools

Hardening

Polymer clay is hardened by baking in an ordinary oven. You must ask an adult to help you with this. DO NOT USE A MICROWAVE OVEN!

Oven temperature should be around 130°C (275°F) but be sure to read the manufacturer's instructions that come with the clay for the correct time and temperature. Put your work on ovenproof dishes to bake. Make sure you allow plenty of time for cooling before you take the clay off the dish. Be patient, it's worth the wait!

Planning

The simplest pieces benefit from some planning at the beginning.

- It helps to start with a picture or a drawing.
- If you are going to put together a lot of similar parts, it's best to make them all at the same time.
- Hardened clay will need glue to stick it to hardened clay.

Safety first

- Wash your hands thoroughly after modelling with polymer clay.
- Make sure any tools or dishes you've borrowed from the kitchen are carefully washed before being used for food again. It's a good idea to ask for special ones to be put aside for clay baking.
- However appetising your model food may look, don't eat it, and don't use modelled plates and dishes for real food.

Animal parade

Let's model some animals.
We've chosen to make an elephant, a piglet, a snail and a little bear. You can choose to make any animals you like.

15
MINUTES

5
MINUTES

You will need:

- *Modelling clay*
- *Modelling tools*
- *Plastic bag and sticky tape*
- *Plastic wobbly eyes (optional)*

What to do...

Prepare your work surface. Choose your colours and get some clay ready in balls. If you want to make eyes for your animals, make sure you've got some black and white clays.

1   Elephant

The elephant has nine pieces. Make the body, tail and four legs. Now make a head and trunk as one piece. Make two ears. Join the legs and tail to the body. Push his head on and curl his trunk up. Press on both his ears. Add his eyes, tweak his tail!

2   Piglet

Piglet is made from eight pieces of clay. Make his head and body from one piece. Flatten one end to make his snout. Use clay tools to mark his mouth and nostrils. Pinch the ear flaps before you fix them on. Don't forget to put a twist in his little tail.

3   Snail

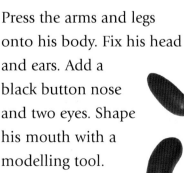

Use four colours to make the snail. Roll out brown, white and black into lengths. Twist the lengths together to make his shell. Use fawn clay for his body. Create his eyes from black and white clay. Make a cut for his mouth. Press the shell onto his body to complete the snail.

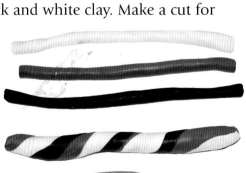

4   Bear

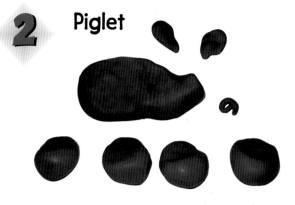

This little bear is made from eight pieces of brown clay, some black for his nose and black and white for his eyes.

Press the arms and legs onto his body. Fix his head and ears. Add a black button nose and two eyes. Shape his mouth with a modelling tool.

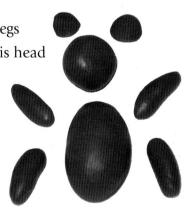

House numbers

Most people need a number on their home so visitors can find them. This is how to make a unique number plate for your home or a gift for a friend.

35 MINUTES

5 MINUTES

You will need:

- *Modelling clay*
- *Modelling tools*
- *Plastic bag*
- *Sticky tape*
- *125mm (5in) circle guide (tin lid will do)*
- *Double-sided sticky pads*
- *Kitchen oven, adult help*

What to do...

Get your work surface ready (see page 4). Think of the colours you would like to use on your house number. Make some clay into balls.

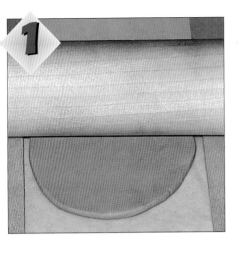

Roll out the clay for the plate about 6mm (0.25in) thick. Use lolly sticks to get the right thickness (see page 5). Cut a circle about 125mm (5in) across using a jar lid or a saucer as a guide.

Work out the size for your numbers, allowing space for a border. Put your numbers in the middle of the background circle and gently press down. Cut some triangular clay shapes in different colours and put

them around the edge. Add dots of clay to the figures if you like them funky! Make sure the back of your plate is flat, then harden the clay (see page 7). When it's cool, put double-sided sticky pads on the back.

Think of all the different styles of numbers you could make! We made some white figures, then decorated them with long strings of green clay.

The black background is about 250 x 100mm (6 x 4in) and it makes the figures stand out well. We made the border by putting some very thin clay onto the edges of the plate.

When you have hardened your house number, let it cool, then put some double-sided sticky pads on the back. Now it's ready for the front door!

Fridge magnets

 **35 MINUTES**

 **5 MINUTES**

12

We made special FRIDGE MAGNETS to stick our shopping lists to the fridge door. They're modelled on our favourite foods, of course!

You will need:

- *Modelling clay*
- *Modelling tools*
- *Plastic bag*
- *Sticky tape*
- *Several flat magnets*
- *Universal glue*
- *Kitchen oven, adult help*

What to do...

Get your work surface ready. Make some clay balls of the colours you are going to use. Think of some fun food items to make. We chose a cup cake and a hot dog!

Create the separate parts from different coloured clays. Find a ridged tool to make the ridges in the paper cup. Assemble carefully.

Make sure the back is flat. When the clay has been hardened (see page 7) and is cool, stick the magnet on with a spot of universal glue.

We made the roll for the hot dog out of two colours, then split it, just like the real thing!

You might like some tomato sauce on yours! How about making your favourite snack?

Leaf dish

25 MINUTES

5 MINUTES

Lots of natural things have interesting shapes and textures. Leaves have veins which you can copy using your clay. Find big leaves with clearly marked veins.

You will need:

- *Modelling clay*
- *Modelling tools*
- *Plastic bag, sticky tape*
- *Lolly sticks, a rolling pin*
- *Natural leaves*
- *Shallow bowl or jar lid*
- *Kitchen oven, adult help*

What to do...

Get your work surface ready and get some clay prepared in a ball (see page 4). The bigger the leaf, the more clay you will need, but also the more impressive will be the result!

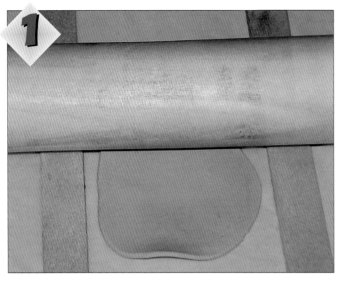

Use a rolling pin to flatten the clay. Put lolly sticks under the rolling pin, as shown, to control the thickness of the clay.

Press the underside of the leaf into the clay. You can gently use the roller to get an even impression.

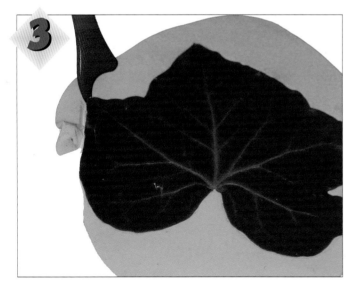

Carefully trim round the leaf with the blade of a modelling tool. Peel the leaf away, leaving the clay leaf shape.

Gently curl up the sides of the clay leaf to form a dish. Put it in a shallow lid to help it keep its shape in the oven as it hardens (see page 7).

Fashion beads

Clay beads have been worn since ancient times. Follow these easy steps to create your own colourful FASHION BEADS collection.

You will need:

- Modelling clay
- Modelling tools, small knife
- Plastic bag, sticky tape
- 2 lolly sticks, a rolling pin
- Cord for stringing beads
- Toothpick, a paper clip
- Kitchen oven, adult help

45 MINUTES

What to do...

Choose bright colours to work with. Follow the steps to make the sort of beads you like. We have made three different kinds. You will need about twenty beads for a full necklace. Harden the beads (see page 7) and leave to cool before threading.

5 MINUTES

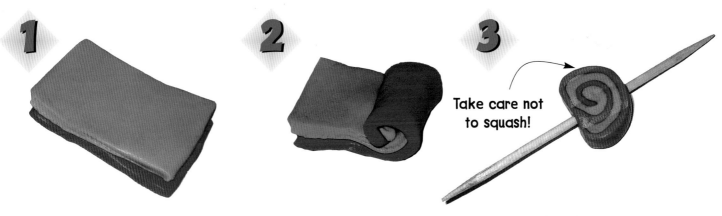

Make two thin strips of clay, 25 x 50mm (1 x 2in). Put one strip over the other.

Roll up both strips together into a tight spiral. Cut 12mm (0.5in) slices with a small knife.

Use a toothpick to make a hole in the bead before hardening.

Take care not to squash!

Cut narrow strips of clay. Place them on a flat strip, 25 x 25mm (1 x 1in) and roll lightly.

Wrap the clay around the thin handle of a paint brush. Join the clay, overlapping a little.

Ease the beads off the handle. After hardening in the oven, the beads will be firm and shiny.

hardened beads

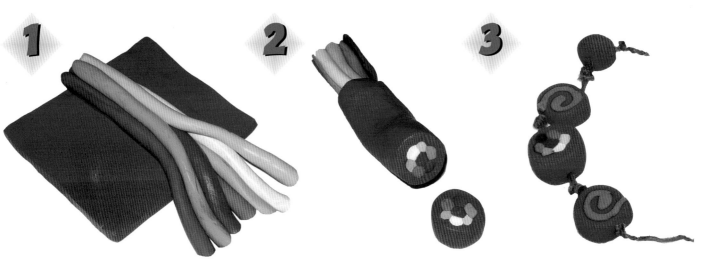

Lay bright-coloured clay rolls on a flat piece of clay. Wrap the clay round, making a cane.

Slice carefully. Make a hole in each bead before hardening.

Make a double knot after each threaded bead. A loop fastens over the bead at the other end.

Friendship bands

To give something as a token of friendship is a great idea. By creating your own beads you can make a different band for each of your friends.

You will need:

- *Modelling clay*
- *Modelling tools, a small knife*
- *Plastic bag, sticky tape*
- *2 lolly sticks, a rolling pin*
- *Shoe lace for stringing beads*
- *Toothpick, paper clip*
- *Kitchen oven, adult help*

35 MINUTES

What to do...

Use colours which look good together. You'll need about fifteen beads to make a wrist band. Make sure your beads have holes before you harden them!

5 MINUTES

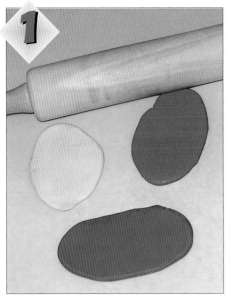

Roll out the clay into thin strips. Put the strips on top of one another.

Trim the pile of strips with a small knife. Cut neat slices to make the beads.

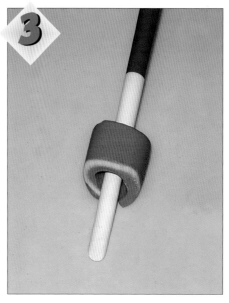

Wrap a slice around a thin handle of a paint brush and overlap the clay to make a join.

You can vary the shape of the beads by making narrow or wide slices. Make round beads by rolling the clay in your hand. Make the hole with a toothpick.

Wrap a three-colour coil around a paint brush handle to make stripy beads. Look at page 17 for other sorts of beads you can make.

reef knot →

Harden the beads and allow them to cool (see page 7). Thread them on a shoe lace. Tie the lace with a simple knot so you can undo it.

Picture frame

35
MINUTES

5
MINUTES

If you find plain picture frames a bit dull, here's a way of making them a bit more fun!

You will need:

- *Modelling clay and tools*
- *Shaped cutters, ruler*
- *Plastic bag, sticky tape*
- *Picture frame*

What to do...

Prepare your work surface. Choose your coloured clays. You'll need most for the flat border pieces. Roll out the clay evenly using the lolly sticks (see page 5).

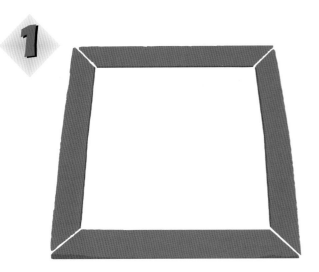

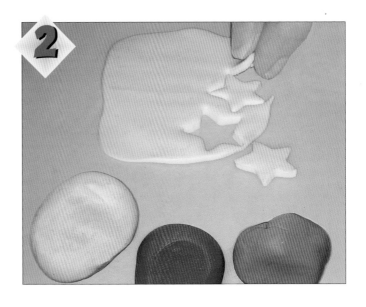

Measure your frame and cut out four pieces of clay to the correct size for the flat border. Make 45° cuts and join the corners. Put the border in place on the frame.

Roll out more clay. Use three or four different clay cutters to make decorative shapes. Plan your design. Work out how many cut-outs of each shape you will need.

Press the shapes gently onto the flat border. Build up the pattern until you have worked all the way around the frame. **Do not harden this piece in the oven**. The clay will dry in the air and harden in time.

Just add a photograph to complete your new frame! You could try decorating a small framed mirror.

Badge boutique

Badges can mean you belong to a group or club. They can also be given as gifts. Try this project and you will be able to make badges for friends and your family.

30 MINUTES

5 MINUTES

You will need:

- Modelling clay and tools
- Shaped cutters
- Plastic bag, sticky tape
- Brooch pins
- Universal glue

What to do...

Think of a badge you'd like to make, or follow one of the methods in the pictures opposite for great results.

When the badges have cooled after hardening (see page 7), fix brooch pins to the backs with universal glue.

Make a base circle about 25mm (1in) across. Use different colours to make the shapes. Petals go around the edge of the base. Mark the edge of the green circle with a matchstick. Add the yellow circle.

Cut a circle for the plate about 40mm (1.5 in) across. Use different colours to make lots of fruit shapes. Place the fruit on the plate and gently press them into place.

Make up each flower shape by curling pieces of flat clay to make petals, then make leaf shapes. Make the base from a small ball of clay. Flatten the back. Add the flowers and leaves to make up your posy.

Cut a moon shape from some rolled out clay. Add a fun face. Badges make ideal gifts for parties and friends.

Desk tidy

This DESK TIDY would make the perfect gift for Mum, Dad or your teacher. It helps keep everybody's desk neat and tidy. This is easily the biggest design we've done, but certainly not the most difficult. Work carefully and your patience be rewarded!

30
MINUTES

5
MINUTES

You will need:

- *Modelling clay and tools*
- *Rolling pin, plastic bag*
- *Kitchen oven, tray*

What to do...

There's lots of rolling out to do, so get your work surface ready.

Roll out two contrasting colours of clay.
For three pots, you will need three oblong
shapes. Use tools to make some zigzag strips
to go round the pots.

Press a zigzag strip onto an oblong shape,
then curl the clay round to make a cylinder.
Use a clay disc for the base. Press the edges of
the clay together to make the pot.

Repeat to make another pot. Put a zigzag strip
round the base. Attach another clay disc
underneath. Gently press the pots together
without squashing the shapes.

Make the third pot the tallest. Place it inside the
shortest. Gently press the pots together. Place
the finished work on an oven-proof tray ready
for hardening (see page 7).

Pencil pals

Here are some fun things to make for yourself and your friends.
They fit on ordinary pencils.

You will need:

- Modelling clay and tools
- Rolling pin, 2 lolly sticks
- Plastic bag, sticky tape
- 3 pencils, 3 pairs wobbly eyes
- Garlic press, glue, kitchen oven
- Universal glue

30 MINUTES

What to do...

You need two colours for each head. We've made three. You can copy these or create similar ones yourself using our method. See page 7 for hardening.

5 MINUTES

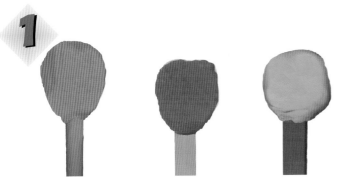

Make the clay into a ball and push the pencil into it, about halfway.

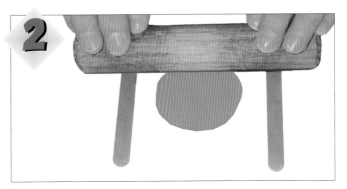

Roll out more clay between lolly-sticks to get an even sheet. Cut out semi-circular shapes and pinch to make ears.

A garlic press makes tiny strings of clay, like hair! Twist two strands together to make horns.

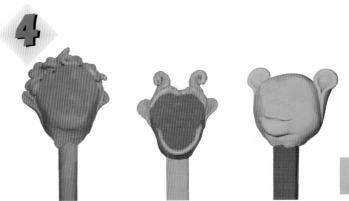

Make ears and press them onto the heads. Put the hair on, one strand at a time. Add the twisted horns and put on the lips.

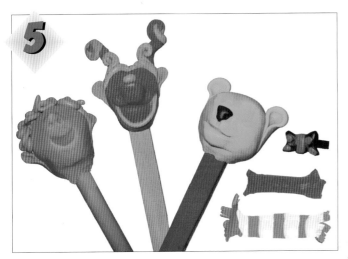

Use clay tools to model the features. Add the noses in different colours. Make a bow tie and scarves. Don't forget the eyes.

When you've finished, gently ease the heads off the pencils. Harden, and, when cool, stick each head back on its pencil with universal glue.

Clay coil pot

Pottery is an ancient craft. Coiling clay was done in prehistoric times! It's a neat way to make a pretty gift for someone you like.

45 MINUTES   **10** MINUTES

You will need:

- *Modelling clay, rolling pin*
- *Modelling tools*
- *1 plastic pot*
- *A plastic bag, tape*
- *Shaped cutters*

What to do...

Find a small empty plastic food container. This will be the support for your pot. You will also be able to use the pot for flowers.
DO NOT harden this item in the oven!

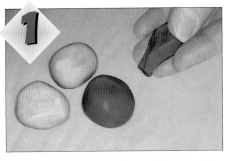

1 Prepare your work surface and some balls of clay. Take some clay and roll it into a sausage.

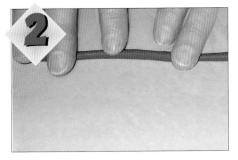

2 Use your whole hand from wrist to fingertips to roll thin coils of clay.

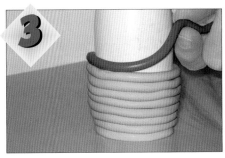

3 Start at the base and wind the clay tightly around the plastic pot. Take care not to flatten the coil. Cover the whole pot.

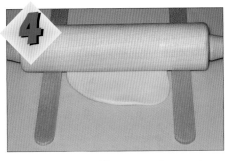

4 Take some different colour clay and roll it out flat.

5 Use a cutter to make shapes to decorate the finished pot!

Once you have wound the coils to the top of the pot, stick the star shapes to the side of the pot. Stick some flowers inside if you like!

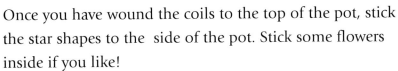

Pebbles

2 MINUTES

10 MINUTES

Here's an idea that's simplicity itself. Pebbles from the beach? Rare stones from faraway places? We started making them from leftover bits, and now we can't stop!

You will need:

• *Modelling clay*

What to do...

Find those bits of clay you thought were too small for anything. Combine colours in flat pieces and strings. Experiment and make sure your finished pebbles are smooth.

Glossary

Baking	Another name for hardening.
Band	A decorative strip of material.
Border	The strip at the edge of something.
Brooch	A piece of jewellery to be worn pinned to the clothing.
Cane	A cane is made by wrapping several rolls of clay of different colours in a flat piece of clay. The result can be sliced. All the slices will have the same pattern.
Consistency	When we work with clay, we want it to be the same quality all the way through. We call this the consistency of the clay.
Contrast	Something appearing sharply different in some way to something else.
Cylinder	A solid shape that has straight sides and a circular section.
Disc	A shape that is round and flat.
Hardening	The process of baking polymer clay is done in an ordinary home oven. The clay becomes much more durable and no longer soft.
Marbling	Streaks of colour like the marks in marble.
Pattern	Pattern can mean many things, but here we usually mean a repeated design.
Polymer clay	Polymer clay is a material based on a kind of plastic. It is called clay because it has many of its qualities and can be put to similar uses.
Roll	A roll is what you get when you roll out clay with your hand on a flat surface.
Section	A section is a slice through something.
Shape cutter	These are made of metal or plastic. They might be bought from craft shops or adapted from other purposes, such as lids.
Texture	What a surface looks or feels like.
Vein	In plants, the patterns on the leaves are called veins.

31

Index